PERMISSION Granted

20 EMPOWERING JOURNAL PROMPTS FOR YOU TO TAKE BACK YOUR POWER AND CHANGE YOUR LIFE

COURTNEY ANDERSON, MSW

Girl on Fire

Omaha, Nebraska

www.girlonfire.biz

Permission Granted / Courtney Anderson - 1st Edition

ISBN 978-0-578-30544-8

CONTENTS

This book is dedicated to any woman who feels unseen, exhausted, shamed, guilty and who desires to change her life in big or small ways, but doesn't always feel like she can. My hope is that this journal will help you feel more empowered, lighter, and wonderfully confident.

How to Use This Journal

Congratulations on taking a step towards caring for yourself. I know that many of you have purchased journals and books, brought them home and maybe never got around to opening, reading, or writing in them. I want this experience to be different for you.

My intention for you is to use this journal to process your thoughts and ideas and maybe some internal struggles too, we all have them. I started writing this journal with the idea of creating thought-provoking journal prompts. Read the personal reflection I have written and then the journal prompt. Reply to the prompt in a way that suits you right now, exactly where you are in your life.

There is so much validation in journaling. Don't be too hard on yourself, journal everyday or occasionally. I prefer to journal when I need to work something out in my head. Journaling gives me the space I need to get the thoughts out of my head and on paper so I can step back and look at them, then take intentional action.

As time passes, what will likely happen when you go back and read your entries, you will see how far you have come, how much you have changed. This is just a piece of the magic of journaling.

After the 20 journal prompts you will see free space. Use these pages to write your own thoughts and ideas. You can change your life; this journal is one of the tools you can use along that journey.

Prompt One

Reflection: I work hard at surrounding myself with likeminded people. But even my most well-intended choices in relationships sometimes turn out to not be that great for me. I have occasionally allowed people's opinions of me and what I am doing influence me. What has been helpful for me in these situations, is for me to slow down and take a closer look at that other person. I have found that most people aren't taking chances, improving their situation or being honest and vulnerable. It has been my experience that people who have judged me aren't the kind of people I really want feedback from. So, I have adopted the manta of "If you are not also doing your own work, your opinion doesn't matter."

Prompt: Is there someone's opinion that I am paying too much attention to? Whose opinions of me matter and whose do not?

Prompt Two

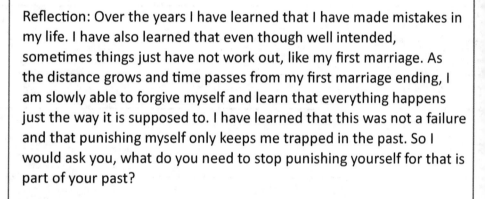

Reflection: Over the years I have learned that I have made mistakes in my life. I have also learned that even though well intended, sometimes things just have not work out, like my first marriage. As the distance grows and time passes from my first marriage ending, I am slowly able to forgive myself and learn that everything happens just the way it is supposed to. I have learned that this was not a failure and that punishing myself only keeps me trapped in the past. So I would ask you, what do you need to stop punishing yourself for that is part of your past?

Prompt: Is today the day I stop punishing myself for my past? What do I need to forgive myself for so that I can make space for my future?

Prompt Three

Reflection: I don't think that as women we give ourselves enough credit for all that we are accomplishing in our lives. My life is so busy and there is so much going on that I forget what I am getting done. For example, I was talking to my son the other morning and he asked me about my college experience. He said to me, "mom, I didn't know you had two college degrees." I sat there in shock, realizing I hadn't been sharing this HUGE part of my life with my sons on a regular basis. Recently, I took some time to look closer at my business revenue. I was comparing the revenue from this year and last year. What I realized was that I had already doubled the revenue I brought in last year. THIS IS A BIG DEAL! I had been so bogged down with the daily meal plans, carpooling, tutoring appointments, and laundry, but I realized I was NOT appreciating my achievements in big and small ways.

Prompt: There is power in glancing back to see how far I have come. What have I accomplished in the last 6 months in my personal and work life?

Prompt Four

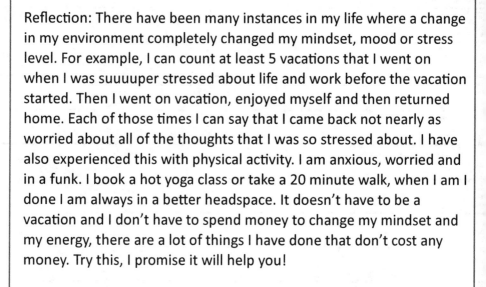

Reflection: There have been many instances in my life where a change in my environment completely changed my mindset, mood or stress level. For example, I can count at least 5 vacations that I went on when I was suuuuper stressed about life and work before the vacation started. Then I went on vacation, enjoyed myself and then returned home. Each of those times I can say that I came back not nearly as worried about all of the thoughts that I was so stressed about. I have also experienced this with physical activity. I am anxious, worried and in a funk. I book a hot yoga class or take a 20 minute walk, when I am I done I am always in a better headspace. It doesn't have to be a vacation and I don't have to spend money to change my mindset and my energy, there are a lot of things I have done that don't cost any money. Try this, I promise it will help you!

Prompt: If I want to shift my energy, I can change my physical environment. What are some ways that I can enhance my environment or shift my energy?

Prompt Five

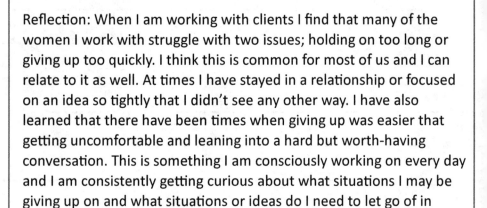

Reflection: When I am working with clients I find that many of the women I work with struggle with two issues; holding on too long or giving up too quickly. I think this is common for most of us and I can relate to it as well. At times I have stayed in a relationship or focused on an idea so tightly that I didn't see any other way. I have also learned that there have been times when giving up was easier that getting uncomfortable and leaning into a hard but worth-having conversation. This is something I am consciously working on every day and I am consistently getting curious about what situations I may be giving up on and what situations or ideas do I need to let go of in order to make space for what serves me?

Prompt: Do I have a pattern of holding on too long? Do I have a pattern of giving up when a situation gets uncomfortable? What are examples of these?

Prompt Six

Reflection: This one is so simple but so effective! I tend to always have a lot of information in my head. I think that this is very common for women, we are responsible for so many things and have thousands of thoughts each day! When I feel anxious, have a lot to get done, feel overwhelmed or stuck, I know that I need to get the information and thoughts from my head out on paper. When in doubt, I brain dump it into a journal. All I do is grab my journal and start to write everything I am thinking and everything I need to get accomplished. I don't judge the order of what I write out or if it makes sense, I just write until I don't have anything else to write. This helps me so much! Then I take a deep breath and pick one item I have written and address it so I can start to see accomplishments and get a small win! And so on....

Prompt: What are all the thoughts in my head right now? Once I write them out, what can I accomplish today?

Prompt Seven

Reflection: I am obsessed with talking about and teaching my clients about boundaries. As a clinical social worker, boundaries are second nature to me. Boundaries are simply how we teach others how to treat us and what is OK and what is NOT OK. The great thing is that I get to decide what is OK and not ok for me and that is very liberating. I have had to set boundaries with friends, colleagues, significant others and family. Boundaries are very healthy and if there is someone in my life who doesn't respect my boundaries I have learned that this is a red flag!

Prompt: What relationships in my life could use some boundaries? What am I currently allowing that I am no longer comfortable with?

Prompt Eight

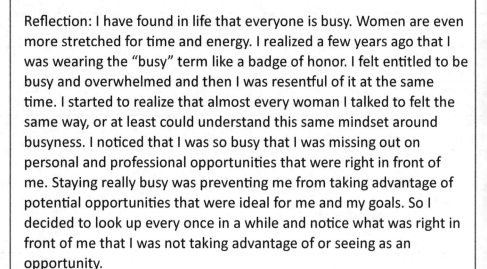

Reflection: I have found in life that everyone is busy. Women are even more stretched for time and energy. I realized a few years ago that I was wearing the "busy" term like a badge of honor. I felt entitled to be busy and overwhelmed and then I was resentful of it at the same time. I started to realize that almost every woman I talked to felt the same way, or at least could understand this same mindset around busyness. I noticed that I was so busy that I was missing out on personal and professional opportunities that were right in front of me. Staying really busy was preventing me from taking advantage of potential opportunities that were ideal for me and my goals. So I decided to look up every once in a while and notice what was right in front of me that I was not taking advantage of or seeing as an opportunity.

Prompt: What potential opportunities are right in front of me that I am not going after or not seeing as potential solutions? How could these opportunities possibly help me achieve my personal and work goals?

Prompt Nine

Reflection: I, like most women, spent a lot of time worrying about what other people think. However, I have realized that the older I get the more I realize that this is generally a waste of valuable time and energy. I want to normalize the fear of judgement, but I also want to move past it. So I have learned that, at the end of the day, my choices are my own. I am also not powerful enough to MAKE anyone else happy or MAKE anyone accept everything that I do. Changing my mindset around judgement has been very healthy for me.

Prompt: What would I do if I knew that no one would judge me for it?

Prompt Ten

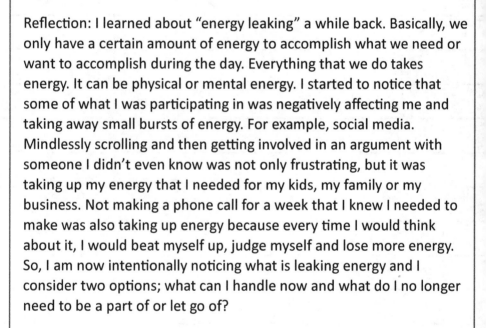

Reflection: I learned about "energy leaking" a while back. Basically, we only have a certain amount of energy to accomplish what we need or want to accomplish during the day. Everything that we do takes energy. It can be physical or mental energy. I started to notice that some of what I was participating in was negatively affecting me and taking away small bursts of energy. For example, social media. Mindlessly scrolling and then getting involved in an argument with someone I didn't even know was not only frustrating, but it was taking up my energy that I needed for my kids, my family or my business. Not making a phone call for a week that I knew I needed to make was also taking up energy because every time I would think about it, I would beat myself up, judge myself and lose more energy. So, I am now intentionally noticing what is leaking energy and I consider two options; what can I handle now and what do I no longer need to be a part of or let go of?

Prompt: What parts of my life are leaking precious energy right now? What can I handle today? What can I let go of?

Prompt Eleven

Reflection: I love and LOATHE social media. I use it for my personal life, but also for my business. I enjoy social media because I have been able to stay connected with so many people from high school, college and beyond. I have also met amazing people on social media that have become real life friends and colleagues. However, in the last year or so I have realized that social media has been causing me more stress and anxiety. It also creates physical pain in my neck, literally! Holding that phone in that position is not good for my body. It has also increased my negative perceptions of people and the world and that is not healthy for me. I have recently drawn a line in the sand and set boundaries with social media and it has really impacted me positively. I went to a reiki practitioner who told me that she felt that I was giving away my power to social media. And guess what? When I started to pull away from and limit my time on social media, the world didn't end and I am ok and so is my business.

Prompt: In what ways is my relationship with social media harmful or beneficial?

Prompt Twelve

Reflection: When I was younger, I used to focus a lot more on the past. I used feel sorry for myself about certain parts of my childhood and what I missed out on due to how I was raised. As I have gotten older, worked with a therapist, worked as a clinical social worker and matured, I have thankfully gotten away from the pity party mentality. I know that everyone has experienced hardships, myself included. But I can say with confidence that there is nothing anyone can do to change the past. But what I can change and impact in the present and the future and that is exciting.

Prompt: To be a forward moving person I need to focus on the present or future.

Do I tend to focus on the past, present or future? How is this affecting my life?

Prompt Thirteen

Reflection: I know that I have not always been kind to myself. I also know that I am not alone in this. So many of the negative things I think about myself are things I would NEVER say to someone else. It is actually a little embarrassing to think about these awful messages that play in my head.....*Who do you think you are? You have gotten so fat, get it together. He is going to leave you and then no one will want you.* I have decided to name these nasty voices in my head "The Shitty Committee" because well, it fits and naming them keeps them separate from the truth.

Prompt: What does the Shitty Committee in my head say to me all day long?

Prompt Fourteen

Reflection: There are times in my life and business when I am doing something and then I realize that I don't even enjoy what I am doing. I mean, I know some things in life HAVE to get done, but for the most part I believe that we have a choice in what we participate in. A few years ago, I was asked to be the PTO vice president. I didn't want to do it, but I reluctantly agreed to do it. And guess what? I did not enjoy it at all. For an entire year I would dread the meetings. At the end of the year I told the rest of the committee that I was not returning, and it was such a relief. That was a painful lesson, knowing that my gut was telling me I didn't want to do it, but I did it anyway and did not enjoy it.

Prompt: What am I doing right now that I dread? What am I doing that I love? What do I want to do more of?

Prompt Fifteen

Reflection: I think that we live in such a busy place these days. Someone is always trying to sell us something and we're always looking for a quick fix to change some part of ourselves. I cannot tell you the money and time that I have wasted trying to change something about myself. The more women I talk to the more I understand that we are all going through this. Even someone that I think is "perfect" or has it all figured out has their own negative thoughts and beliefs about themselves. Instead of looking externally for someone or something to fix me, I have learned to get quiet and consider changing those thoughts and flooding my mind with radical self-love.

Prompt: *There is nothing wrong with me. What can I do today to show myself love and understanding?*

Prompt Sixteen

Reflection: The way I speak about myself has a direct effect on my outcomes, my mental health and my self-image. A few years ago, I learned about the power of words. More specifically, the words we use to talk about ourselves. I began to see that women were bashing themselves left and right. I was also doing it myself and I decided that it was critically important for me to intentionally change the way I talked about myself, right away!

Prompt: How often am I qualifying something about myself with a negative word? For example, I am terrible at exercising, or I am bad at being organized? How can I change my words to lift myself up?

Prompt Seventeen

Reflection: Who I allow into my life is my choice. Who I surround myself with is entirely up to me. I heard this concept a few years ago, that I am the average sum of the 5 people that I spend the most time with. So I decided to get clear on who I was allowing into my life. I noticed that some of the people were very negative and had a toxic mindset. That was starting to distract me from achieving a better life for myself and my sons. I made the intentional decision that I would surround myself with people who supported me, not with people who made me feel terrible. Life became easier and more enjoyable when I was sharing it with likeminded people.

Prompt: Who is currently in my life that lifts me up and supports me? What are the qualities I want people in my life to have?

Prompt Eighteen

Reflection: A while back I started to be asked to facilitate trainings and classes for other female entrepreneurs. One of the things that was incredibly common was that women were telling me that they were doing so many things that they felt that they "should" do for one reason or another. I started to play around with this and landed on a simple, but effective thought to teach and work through. So I started to teach that with each scenario that comes up consider this: What do I think I should do in this situation and then what do I need to do? What happens is that the answer to the NEED was what was the most authentic and desired choice. I use this myself every day and it really does help me to process my thoughts and choices.

Prompt: In what areas of my life can I ask myself, "Am I choosing to do what I think I SHOULD do or am I doing what I NEED to do? What do I need in this very moment?"

Prompt Nineteen

Reflection: In my own personal journey and in working with my clients, I have learned so much about progress. I realized about 7 years ago that I was spending A LOT of my time and energy trying to help everyone else, give them advice, and want more for them. In hindsight I see that this was distracting me from dealing with my own problems and dysfunctional relationships. I learned the hard way that I couldn't change anyone else and that I had sacrificed my own happiness time and time again by putting myself on the back burner.

Prompt: Where in my life do I need to start minding my own business? Where in my life do I need to start to stand up for myself?

Prompt Twenty

Reflection: Trust me on this one. I know from personal experience that physical clutter stresses me out. When I am trying to focus and accomplish a task that needs my attention and there is physical clutter around me, I find it harder to focus. I started to notice this with my clients as well. I started to see a pattern. What I found was that there is a direct correlation between physical clutter and mind clutter. Meaning, that extra "stuff" this is strewn all over, not put away and too much of it, makes for a cluttered, stressed, and overwhelmed mind. The external clutter in my physical environment is a direct reflection of any clutter that is in my mind. I have committed to donating, selling, or gifting items I no longer use or value. I tidy my workspace so that I have at least one sanctuary in my home to ensure that I can focus and not feel stressed when I need to accomplish my work.

Prompt: What does my physical environment look like? How does my physical environment make me feel? Is clutter a problem in my home and how can I address it?

"In any situation, you have the right, power
and ability to choose your experience."
Iyanla Vanzant

"The truth will set you free, but first it will piss you off."
Gloria Steinem

"You may not control all of the events that happened to you, but
you can decide not to be reduced by them."
Maya Angelou

"And the day came when the risk to remain tight in a bud
was more painful than the risk it took to blossom."
Anais Nin

"Tell me what it is that you plan to do with your
one wild and precious life?"
Mary Oliver

"You've got to learn to leave the table
when love's no longer being served."
Nine Simone

"The most common way people give up their power
is thinking they don't have any."
Alice Walker

"Loving ourselves through the process of owning our story Is the
bravest thing we will ever do."
Brene Brown

About the Author

Courtney Anderson is a clinical social worker and life coach for women, and the founder of Girl On Fire. Her mission is help women learn the origins of their patterns and give them the tangible tools to change their lives. She holds BSW degree from the University of Nebraska at Omaha and a master's degree in clinical social work from Florida State University, and has appeared on multiple podcasts, NPR, CNN and was featured in the NY Times and Tampa Bay Times. She lives in Omaha with her husband and two sons.

CPSIA information can be obtained
at www.ICGtesting.com
Printed in the USA
LVHW010106020422
714993LV00009B/494